Can I Ask You a Question?

Can I Ask You a Question?

THOUGHT CATALOG

THOUGHT CATALOG Books

BROOKLYN, NY

THOUGHT
CATALOG
Books

Published by Thought Catalog Books, a division of The Thought & Expression Co., Williamsburg, Brooklyn. Founded in 2010, Thought Catalog is a website and imprint dedicated to your ideas and stories. We publish fiction and non-fiction from emerging and established writers across all genres. For general information and submissions: manuscripts@thoughtcatalog.com.

First edition, 2017

ISBN: 978-1542904803

Printed and bound in the United States.

10 9 8 7 6 5 4 3 2 1

Contents

Your One-Word Answer To These 50 Questions Will Reveal Exactly Who You Are

Kendra Syrdal

1. What's the first thing you grab for in the morning?

2. Who is your biggest inspiration in life?

3. What do you think people notice most about you?

4. Who do you *hope* people notice most about you?

5. What is your biggest weakness/fatal flaw?

6. What is your biggest strength?

7. What to you is the perfect, most ideal age to be?

8. High school. Awesome or terrible?

9. Cats or dogs?

10. Adjective that best describes you when you're drunk?

11. Why do you love your best friend so much?

12. Where do you want to go more than any other place in the world?

13. Beaches or snow?

14. What is your absolute, number one, biggest pet peeve?

15. What is one personality trait you simply have no time for?

16. Zodiac, MBTI, or Birth Order? Which is the one you lean towards?

17. Do you believe in something after death?

18. How does someone instantaneously get on your good side?

19. How about your bad side?

20. How do you hope you're described by people when you're not around?

21. What is your least favorite attribute about yourself?

22. Is it okay to sleep with socks on?

23. Coffee or tea?

24. How many dates until you feel like it's okay to have sex with someone?

25. What is your love language?

26. Do you or do you not believe in ghosts?

27. What's your vice?

28. Twitter, Facebook, or Instagram?

29. Favorite artist?

30. Odd numbers or even numbers?

31. Do you believe in organizing or life or letting things just happen?

32. Are you more right brained or left brained?

33. Which do you prefer, logic or creativity?

34. Do you think opposites truly attract?

35. What is your Hogwarts house?

36. Ask for permission or ask for forgiveness?

37. Do you think chemistry is instant or grows with time?

38. Do you trust someone until proven otherwise or do you think trust has to be earned no matter who with?

39. Are there situations in which you think lying is okay and understandable?

40. Comfortable silences or non-stop conversation?

41. Do you believe in fate or do you think we're in complete control over our circumstances?

42. Love or money?

43. Impulsive or methodical?

44. Are you pro-technology/constantly connected or do you think digital detoxes are super necessary?

45. Do you think it's better to have loved and lost than to have never loved at all?

46. Do you question things even if it will bother someone or do you try to not rock the boat?

47. TV shows or Movies?

48. Books or Magazines?

49. Which is more preferable—being nice or being fair?

50. Describe what would bring you the ultimate happiness in life.

16 Questions That Will Show You Who You Are (And What You're Meant To Do)

Brianna Wiest

Understanding who we are has less to do with discovery and more to do with remembrance than is typically understood. Have you ever had a realization that didn't precede a laundry list of examples, isolated moments and meaningless experiences and random relationships that compile to reveal a pattern or truth? Probably not.

The real work of anything is simply becoming conscious of what is already true.

The essential point of a psychological guidance system (religious or not)—rather, the kinds that *work*—is not to supplant a mindset into you. Rather, to give you the tools for introspection, to figure out the answers yourself. To pose questions, give examples, have you reflect and through that recognition connect to *your* inner guidance system, your intuition, your essential self.

I say this with complete sincerity: the answers to these questions are some that have (literally) changed the course of my life. I'd be remiss not to have compiled and shared them. So here you go, the 16 most important questions you will ever ask yourself:

1. What, and who, is worth suffering for?

2. What would you stand for if you knew that nobody would judge you?

3. What would you do if you knew that nobody would judge you?

4. Based on your daily routines, where will you be in five years? Ten? 20?

5. Who do you admire most, and why?

6. What do you not want anybody else to know about you?

7. What are a few things you thought you would never get over while you were going through them? Why did they seem so insurmountable? How did you?

8. What are your greatest accomplishments so far?

9. What would be too good to believe, if someone were to sit down and tell you what's coming next in your life?

10. Who from your past are you still trying to earn the acceptance of?

11. If you didn't have to work anymore, what would you do with your days?

12. What are the five most common things in your daily routine (aside from the basics, such as eating and sleeping?)

13. What do you wish those five most common things were instead?

14. If you really believed you didn't have control over something, you'd accept it as matter-of-fact. What do you struggle to accept that you have "no control" over? What part of you makes you think or hope otherwise?

15. If you were to walk through your home and put your hand on every single thing you own, how many of them would make you sincerely feel happy or at peace? Why do you keep the rest?

16. What bothers you most about other people? What do you love most in other people? What bothers you most about yourself? What do you love most about yourself? (Dig until you see the correlation).

50 Questions That Will Help You Find Your Way In Life When You're Lost

Heidi Priebe

1. What makes me feel wide-awake, even when I'm lacking sleep?

2. What makes me feel exhausted, even when I'm perfectly well rested?

3. In twenty years, how will I look back on this period of my life?

4. In twenty years, how will I look back on this period of my life if it stays exactly the way it is now for the next five years?

5. What is something I've always wanted to do, but haven't yet?

6. What advice would my ten-year-old self give me?

7. If someone I look up to took over my life, what major changes would they make?

8. What have I always admired, but assumed I wasn't naturally talented enough to try?

9. Why do I assume other people can be wildly successful, but I can't be?

10. Which traits do all of the people I look up to have in common?

11. During the best period of my life, what was going right for me?

12. During the worst period of my life, what was I lacking?

13. If I were eighteen years old again, which life path would I pick for myself, knowing what I know now?

14. What's holding me back from picking that life path now?

15. Am I more worried about proving my enemies wrong about me, or proving my friends right?

16. Since there'll be challenges along any path I choose, which problems am I happiest to have?

17. In which ways do I self-sabotage and why?

18. If I died today, what would my biggest regret be?

19. What do I desperately want but won't admit to myself (hint:

it's the thing that instantly came to mind when you read this, which you immediately silenced and pushed away).

20. When do I feel the most attractive?

21. When do I feel the least attractive?

22. Which feelings am I constantly running away from in life?

23. What might those feelings tell me about myself if I stopped and actually listened to them?

24. What do I do when I'm procrastinating?

25. What have I willingly gone above and beyond for in the past?

26. What makes me incredibly angry, and what core fear is that anger protecting me from?

27. A year from now, what would I like my life to look like?

28. What is something I can start doing today that would make my life radically different in a year?

29. How might other people describe my character?

30. How would I like other people to describe my character?

31. When am I the most present in my environment?

32. Which major mistakes have I seen others make that I never want to make myself?

33. If I knew I'd never be recognized for my work, which work would I do anyway?

34. Under which conditions do I allow myself to feel loved?

35. Under which conditions do I allow myself to feel happy?

36. If I knew for sure that my life would stay exactly the way it is forever unless I changed something, what would I change?

37. Am I secretly just waiting around hoping a miracle (or another person) will show up and save me from my problems?

38. What makes me feel grounded in life?

39. What makes me feel scared?

40. What might I find on the other side of that fear?

41. If I put aside my successes, my belongings and my relationships, what words would I use to define myself?

42. If everyone I were trying to impress in life dropped dead tomorrow, what would I do with my life (besides cry over their deaths).

43. When do I feel the most proud of myself?

44. When do I feel the most ashamed of myself?

45. What would I do if shame were not in the picture?

46. If I were to abandon everything I have now and start over anew, what would I miss the most about my current life?

47. Which major life issues have I surmounted in the past and what helped me surmount them?

48. What has gone unexpectedly right for me in life?

49. All conditions aside, what do I want to see happen?

50. At the end of my life, what will I regret never having given a shot?

4

25 Powerful Questions To Ask Yourself Daily That Will Bring You A Bit Of Clarity

Rezzan Hussey

There's nothing like asking ourselves powerful questions to cut through it and help us to see what's really going on.

Actually, in terms of high impact self-reflection, questions are pretty tough to beat.

The reason for that is, questions are unique in among the other contemplative practices because when you ask yourself a question, your brain has to answer: it can't leave that shiz hanging. It could be a day, two days, a week; that response is gonna come.

And the better the quality of the powerful questions you ask, the more real you can get with yourself. Or as Tony Robbins says "Successful people ask better questions, and as a result, they get better answers."

So what are some powerful questions that you can ask yourself at the beginning, middle and end of each day?

Beginning Of Day Powerful Questions

How am I feeling right now?

Did I wake up on the wrong side? Is it the wrong side, every single day? If so, what's up with that?

Is there a longing that I have that is going unattended to? What am I avoiding? Am I giving enough attention to my bedtime routine and sleep quality? Did I go to bed telling myself a negative story about life?

How am I feeling about this day ahead?

What am I looking forward to and not looking forward to? Is there anything I am excited about? Dreading? What is the source of the excitement and dread?

Does this question make me feel uncomfortable/irritated? What is the source of that discomfort and irritation?

Do I feel neither 'here nor there' about the day? How does apathy feel in my body?

What am I saying no to?

What aspects of the day or myself am I already in resistance to? Did I find fault in the person in the mirror? Just what is the purpose of that inner critic?

What can I accept that I can't change?

What aspect of my current circumstances isn't optimal, and that's putting it nicely. Can I choose it anyway?

What is the most important (not urgent) thing that I do?

Which parts of the day require my total presence? Who is it important that I come through for? Why is it important?

What have I agreed to do, that I do not want to do?

Have I agreed to spend the time in a way that I would rather not? Why did I do that? Are they 'good' reasons (I'm lending a hand) or 'bad' reasons (I felt pushed into it)?

Who is judging what's good and what's bad?

Who do I need to be for this day to work?

Do I need to be productive and focused? Do I need to be patient, kind and gentle?

What can I do today that will be a unique expression of me?

Who can I call and have an honest chat with? What can I do for me and my health? What small actions can I take in my personal projects? What can I learn that I care about knowing?

How can I be more of 'me' at work and at home?

What small steps can I take to show that I am serious about loving myself?

What five or ten-minute actions can I take that will move me towards the future of my wildest dreams?

What would scare me slightly, that I could do today?

What small thing would represent a victory over myself? Could I chat to the cute waitress? Could I notice what's going on around me more? Could I create some space in the day to be left alone with my thoughts?

Check-ins

Where is my attention going right now?

Am I being present to my tasks? If not, where are my thoughts going? What effects is that having? Is there anything I need to learn from that?

How am I not being generous (with my time/words/presence)?

Am I holding back on my work or other people? If so, why?

How am I feeling right now?

What is my emotional state in this moment? Am I feeling relaxed and calm? Slightly nervous/anxious? What sensations accompany these feelings?

How is my breathing?

Is my breathing shallow and upper respiratory, or full bodied? Am I holding my breath right now?

Powerful Questions To Ask At The End Of The Day

What was the most important thing I did today?

Did I give someone my presence and attention when it was needed? Did I get to that barre class even though I really couldn't be bothered? Did I say no when I needed to? Did I stifle a moan/pull to argue and find a more empowering way of being?

What gave me the most joy today?

Maybe the same things as above. Maybe just your morning bagel.

What caused me the most conflict and stress?

Why was it stressful? Why really? What's the story I am telling myself?

What am I grateful for?

Record five things.

Do I need to clear anything up?

Did I say something that wasn't truthful, or compassionate, or both? Do I need to apologize for anything? What did I not say that I need to say?

What did I learn?

Did the course of the day highlight any perspective/behavioral shifts needed?

What do I need to let go?

You could accompany this one with a little sing song.

101 Questions Girls Would Actually Want To Be Asked On A First Date

Kendra Syrdal

1. What were you like as a little kid?

2. Who are you closest to in your family?

3. Who do you think you're most like in your family?

4. What's your favorite memory from growing up?

5. What was your favorite subject in school?

6. Tell me about your best friend.

7. Why did you choose the college you chose?

8. What to you is a "perfect" day?

9. Which would be harder for you to give up: coffee or alcohol?

10. If you could trade lives with one person for an entire day who would it be and why?

11. What is something you wish people asked you more often?

12. If you were a stereotypical character in a movie, who would you be?

13. What is the movie you tell everyone is your favorite, and what is your *actual* favorite?

14. What was the last book you read that really resonated with you?

15. Pizza or wine?

16. Salty or sweet?

17. Summer or Fall?

18. What's your favorite holiday that isn't Christmas or your birthday?

19. If you could find out the truth to one unsolved mystery, which would you pick and why?

20. What is your favorite thing to do?

21. What is your favorite feature about yourself?

22. What's the dumbest thing you're afraid of?

23. What is the best gift you've ever received?

24. What is a TV show you can quote every line from?

25. What are you really, really good at?

26. Do you think you'd want to be famous?

27. If yes, how do you think you'd handle it?

28. What's your superpower?

29. What superpower would you want?

30. What is your favorite quote?

31. What is a song that you can't help but sing along to whenever you hear it?

32. How would you describe yourself in just five words?

33. What makes you laugh the hardest?

34. Who is your favorite TV couple that you think of when you think of "relationship goals"?

35. Why are you in the field that you're in?

36. What do you love most about your job?

37. What do you like the least about it?

38. What is your most bizarre talent?

39. What's your karaoke go to?

40. Who is the one person in this world that knows you best?

41. What do you love to do on your days off?

42. Do you think money really buys happiness?

43. So what is happiness to you?

44. What is something you've never done that you've always wanted to do?

45. Have you ever fought with a stranger online about something?

46. What to you is the perfect way to spend a weekend?

47. Tell me about the best party you've ever been to.

48. Is there a documentary or book that really changed the way you thought about something?

49. How do you think you'd fair in the Hunger Games?

50. What commercials make you cry?

51. What do you think is the most fun part about dating?

52. And what's the worst part about dating?

53. How do you want people to remember you?

54. Are you a dog person or a cat person?

55. What's your Patronus?

56. What is your favorite part about the city you live in?

57. What would you want your obituary to say?

58. What's your go-to Tinder bio?

59. How do you want to die?

60. What is one thing you feel your life is missing?

61. What's the craziest thing you've ever done?

62. What was the coolest part about where you grew up?

63. Tell me about how you became close with one of your best friends.

64. What's your weirdest/quirkiest habit?

65. What's one piece of advice you think everyone needs to live by?

66. If I asked your co-workers to describe you, what would they say?

67. What about your best friends?

68. How about your parents?

69. What do you think makes you unique from other people?

70. Where is the coolest place you've ever been to on a vacation?

71. If you weren't doing what you're doing now as a career, what would you want to be doing?

72. Who has had the biggest influence on your life?

73. Tell me about your childhood pets.

74. Who was your favorite teacher?

75. What was the dumbest thing you did in college?

76. What's something that, try as you might, you just can't do?

77. Were you popular in high school?

78. What's your favorite word?

79. What's your guilty pleasure?

80. If you could be best friend with any famous person, dead or alive, who would it be?

81. What's your favorite memory ever?

82. When do you feel most yourself?

83. What would your *Shark Tank* idea be?

84. Who is a celebrity that drives you absolutely crazy?

85. What's the most spontaneous thing you've ever done?

86. What makes you nervous?

87. What are some of your ambitions in life?

88. Have an Tinder nightmare stories?

89. Do you consider yourself more of an introvert or an extrovert?

90. What makes you the most angry?

91. How do you feel about confrontation?

92. Who would play you in a movie about your life?

93. How did your parents pick your name?

94. What would you save first if your apartment caught on fire?

95. If you could change the decade you were born into, what would you change it to?

96. What's the best part about your typical week?

97. Do you prefer to live alone or with roommates?

98. What's the weirdest thing that pops up if I Google you?

99. Who do you call when you have big news?

100. What are you dying to ask me?

101. Can I get you another drink?

6

50 Questions To Ask A Girl If You Want To Know Who She Really Is

Nicole Tarkoff

1. What's one thing that's happened to you that has made you a stronger person?

2. What's one thing that's happened to you in your life that made you feel weak?

3. Where is one place you feel most like yourself?

4. Where is your favorite place to escape to?

5. Who do you think has had the largest influence on the person you are today?

6. If you could change one thing about yourself what would it be?

7. If you had one day left to live, what would you do first?

8. What decade do you feel you most belong in?

9. Who are you closest to in your family? Why?

10. Who is the one person in this world that knows you best?

11. What is your favorite quality about your best friend?

12. When you were younger what did you think you were going to be when you grew up?

13. If you could identify with one fictional character (from a book, show, or movie) who would it be?

14. Do you easily accept compliments? Or do you hate compliments?

15. Is your favorite attribute about yourself physical or non-physical?

16. What is your favorite physical attribute about yourself?

17. What is your favorite non-physical attribute about yourself?

18. Do you believe in love at first sight?

19. Do you believe in soul mates?

20. How seriously do you take horoscopes?

21. Have you ever been in love? How many times?

22. What makes you fall in love with someone?

23. What does vulnerability mean to you? What has the ability to make you vulnerable?

24. What's one thing you're scared to ask a man, but really want to?

25. If you were a man for a day, what would be the first thing you do?

26. What do you find most attractive about each sex?

27. What's one thing you'd love to learn more about?

28. What is something you've never done that you've always wanted to do?

29. Why haven't you done it yet?

30. If money didn't matter, what would your dream job be?

31. If you had off from work today, what would you do?

32. What was the last thing that made you cry?

33. What was the last thing that made you laugh?

34. What is your favorite memory?

35. What's the last thing that REALLY embarrassed you?

36. What is your biggest fear?

37. Do you have any regrets? What's your biggest one?

38. Have you ever broken a law? If you haven't what is one law you'd love to break?

39. What is the craziest thing you've ever done?

40. Would you have a conversation with a stranger?

41. Would you tell a stranger they have toilet paper hanging from their shoe? Or their dress tucked into their underwear? (Or anything else that is embarrassing to be seen in public)?

42. What's your favorite joke?

43. Are you a dog person or a cat person?

44. If you could be any animal, what animal would you be?

45. What's one show, movie, or book, you're embarrassed to admit you enjoy?

46. How do you think your parents would describe you as a child?

47. If you could go back to any age or time of your life, what age or time would it be?

48. What's something you believe in that not everyone else does?

49. What's one thing you would say that makes you unique from other people?

50. What is one thing you feel your life is missing?

7

50 'Would You Rather' Questions That Will Tell You What Kind Of Man He Really Is

Erin Cossetta

1. Would you rather end up with someone smarter than you, or someone more successful than you?

2. Would you rather travel to a new city with your phone battery on 10% and no charger or only $100 in your pocket?

3. Would you rather rather give or receive a lap dance?

4. Would you rather be an exceptional stay at home parent, or an average office worker?

5. Would you rather have an unlimited amount of money or sex?

6. Would you rather be able to pay for everyone in your family to own their house outright, or travel the world alone for one year?

7. Would you rather have an awesome reputation, but secretly be a shitty person, or have everyone think you're a shitty person but actually be awesome?

8. Would you rather turn bright purple every time you lied, or not be able to have sex for 24 hours every time you lied?

9. Would you rather be able to speak every language fluently or be able to stream any TV show or movie ever made whenever and wherever you want?

10. Would you rather lose your penis or lose your mind?

11. Would you rather show up to work naked for a full day or make everyone in your office show up naked for a full day while you wear clothes?

12. Would you rather be super smart or super rich?

13. Would you rather be considered a perfect 10 in terms of attractiveness, or date someone who is considered a perfect 10?

14. Would you rather be able to give or receive earth-shattering orgasms on command?

15. Would you rather date Princess Diana or Kate Upton?

16. Would you rather think the best of people and be wrong or think the worst of people and be right?

17. Would you rather have pancake-sized nipples and a gigantic penis, or normal sized nipples and a normal penis?

18. Would you rather have one million dollars and never eat meat for the rest of your life, or continue to eat meat?

19. Would you rather be the age you are now forever, or know you'll only live another 20 years?

20. Would you rather be able to talk to all dogs or read the mind of any one woman you choose?

21. Would you rather only be able to do one sexual position for the rest of your life, or be able to do unlimited positions, but it has to be a different woman each time?

22. Would you rather be super happy or super rich?

23. Would you rather wear yoga pants every day for the rest of your life or a dress for one year?

24. Would you rather have your own talk show or publish your memoir?

25. Would you rather ONLY be able to rap or lose the ability to speak?

26. Would you rather have a domesticated pet bear or a domesticated pet tiger?

27. Would you rather have an unlimited amount of puppies or french fries?

28. Would you rather only be able to have oral for the rest of your life, or only be able to do missionary?

29. Would you rather live in a modest home in an expensive city, or an expensive home in a modest city?

30. Would you rather stop aging at 25 or have $10,000 every year?

31. Would you rather host SNL or the next presidential debate where you make all the rules?

32. Would you rather be super attractive or super intelligent?

33. Would you rather be on top or have your partner be on top?

34. Would you rather be with someone who's overly confident or overly insecure?

35. Would you rather pick out lingerie for your partner or have them surprise you?

36. Would you rather date someone 10 years older or 10 years younger than you?

37. Would you rather have your partner only scream or only whisper during sex?

38. Would you rather have romantic lighting during sex or romantic music?

39. Would you rather be able to hear your partners thoughts during sex one time or have them hear your thoughts one time?

40. Would you rather watch porn or read sexy messages from your partner?

41. Would you rather be extremely famous for something you don't care that much about, or just known locally for something you're very proud of?

42. Would you rather live in a fancy high rise or a fancy McMansion?

43. Would you rather believe everything in the Bible is true or everything in *Twilight* is true?

44. Would you rather have a sex slave or be someone's sex slave?

45. Would you rather have a lifetime supply of tacos or pizza?

46. Would you rather be really good looking with your clothes on and ugly with your clothes off or vice versa?

47. Would you rather be Brad Pitt or Barack Obama?

48. Would you rather be in the apocalypse of *Armageddon* or *The Walking Dead*?

49. Would you rather have unlimited time or unlimited money?

50. Would you rather be with someone who you know loves you more than you love them or vice versa?

8

50 Deep First Date Questions That'll Put Your Chemistry To The Test

Holly Riordan

1. What do you hate the most about modern dating?

2. Has a book ever changed your life?

3. Do you believe in love at first sight or do you think it's bullshit?

4. If aliens came to Earth, would you be scared of them or would you welcome them?

5. Has a song ever made you cry?

6. Why do you get up in the morning?

7. What's the most inspirational saying you've ever heard?

8. What's the worst thing that you've ever done?

9. If you could rewind time, what one moment would you want to relive?

10. If you were famous, would you still want a relationship or would you sleep around?

11. If you were free to murder one person without getting punished, would you?

12. Do you think people are born good or born evil?

13. Have you ever had a near-death experience?

14. Would you rather be hideous or illiterate?

15. Have you ever had your heart broken?

16. What's the sweetest gift you've ever given your mother?

17. What was the first thing you masturbated to?

18. Are you proud to tell people about your job or embarrassed about what you do?

19. Do you think an animal's life is just as valuable as a human's life?

20. Has a celebrity's death ever caused you to cry?

21. Do you resent your exes or do you wish them well?

22. If you got a girl pregnant, would you consider it a burden or a blessing?

23. Do you like what you see when you look in the mirror?

24. Have you ever written poetry? What about song lyrics?

25. Who would you call if you only had moments left to live?

26. Do you believe in magic?

27. Do you believe in the afterlife?

28. Do you usually go with your gut or with your brain?

29. What celebrity do you think deserves more attention?

30. Have you ever questioned your sexuality?

31. Is there anyone in this world that you genuinely hate?

32. Would the childhood version of you look up to the current version of you?

33. How are you going to leave your mark on the world?

34. Would you lie to keep your best friend out of prison?

35. What type of imaginary scenarios do you create in your head?

36. What's the earliest memory you have of life?

37. What's the most important thing on your bucket list?

38. Do you consider yourself to be a good person?

39. Do you think you have a purpose in life?

40. Do you think you'd be capable of murder?

41. Do you believe men and women can "just" be friends?

42. Are you following your dreams or have you given up on them?

43. Which gender stereotype about men do you hate the most?

44. If you could erase specific memories from your mind, would you?

45. Do you love your pets as much as you love your human family members?

46. Have you ever seen a ghost? If not, do you believe they exist?

47. Which fictional character do you relate the most to?

48. Would you choose to live forever if you had the opportunity?

49. Who was your hero when you were a little kid?

50. How do you feel about me?

9

25 Questions That Will Tell You Immediately Whether He's 'One Of The Good Ones'

Jason Motta

1. If you had a magic watch that would bring you back to any moment in your life and give you a do-over, what would you change?

2. What do you want to do differently than your parents?

3. How would you want your hypothetical children to turn out different than you?

4. How would you spend your free time if you could be invisible whenever you wanted?

5. What do you think prevents most people from being happy?

6. What's something that has happened to you that has fundamentally changed your personality?

7. What's different about you compared to most people?

8. Do you think people get better over time, or are we born the kind of person we're always going to be?

9. What makes a person 'weak'?

10. What do you think the best age is?

11. If you kept a diary and the people close to you read it one day, would they be surprised about what you really think?

12. What's a character flaw that you can't stand?

13. What do you think prevents most people from being successful?

14. If your apartment building was on fire and you had time to save three things before it burned down, what would you pick?

15. What's an example of a 'victimless crime'?

16. What animal do you most admire, and why?

17. Who is a fictional character that you've really related to?

18. What kind of old person will you be?

19. What would make you the most disappointed to hear about your (hypothetical) child?

20. How do you hope people describe you?

21. Do you believe in karma?

22. What kind of qualities make a good politician?

23. What do the people in your family all have in common?

24. What do you hope to change about yourself as you get older?

25. Do you think it takes two people to make a toxic relationship—or are some people just crazy?

10

50 Deep Questions To Ask Your Boyfriend Tonight That Will Immediately Bring You Two Closer

Nicole Tarkoff

1. What did you think when you first met me?

2. What do you remember most about the night/day we first met?

3. What about our relationship makes you really happy?

4. How long did you think our relationship would last when we first started dating?

5. If you had one word to describe our relationship what would it be?

6. If you had one word to describe our love what would it be?

7. What's your biggest fear for this relationship?

8. Do you believe there's one person you're 'meant' to be with?

9. Do you believe in fate? destiny?

10. What's one difference between us that you absolutely love?

11. What's one similarity between us that you absolutely love?

12. What about me made you fall in love?

13. Is love something that scares you?

14. What about love scares you?

15. What's your favorite memory of us?

16. What's one thing you want to do together that we've never done before?

17. If something happened where I had to move very far away, would you attempt long-distance? Or go our separate ways?

18. Where is your favorite place to be with me?

19. What's one thing you're scared to ask me, but really want to know the answer to?

20. What's one thing you feel our relationship is lacking?

21. What's your favorite non-physical quality about me?

22. What's your favorite physical quality about me?

23. If our relationship ended, what's the one thing about it you'd miss the most?

24. Do you think you've been vulnerable in our relationship?

25. What do you think was your most vulnerable moment in our relationship?

26. Do you think I've been vulnerable in our relationship?

27. What do you think has been the hands-down funniest moment since we started dating?

28. What's one quality about me that I see as a flaw that you absolutely love?

29. What's one secret you've wanted to tell me, but haven't?

30. Do you think there's such thing as the 'right' person for you?

31. Do you think I'm the 'right' person for you? (If yes) What about me makes me the 'right' person?

32. If I said you could date other people, would you?

33. What do you think I'd say is your most attractive quality?

34. What's your favorite way to show affection?

35. What's your favorite way to receive affection?

36. What's one thing you think makes our relationship unique from everyone else's?

37. If you could change one thing about our relationship what would it be?

38. If we could go anywhere together right now, where would you want to go?

39. What do you think is your biggest strength in this relationship?

40. What's your biggest weakness in this relationship?

41. Who do you think is the most affectionate in our relationship?

42. How do you think we both have changed since we first started dating?

43. What about us both is exactly the same since we first started dating?

44. What's one thing I do that makes you feel good, that you wish I did more?

45. What's one thing about your life you would never change for someone else, including me?

46. What about us do you think works well together? How do we balance each other out?

47. What's one thing you hope happens in the future of our relationship?

48. What does love mean to you?

49. What do I mean to you?

50. What does this relationship mean to you?

11

31 Scarily Deep Questions You May Be Intimidated To Ask Your Partner (But Should Anyway)

Kendra Syrdal

Relationships can be tricky…I know, *I know*. Not only a *Scrubs* quote but also the most OBVIOUS statement to make ever. The thing about dating in the 20-teens is that it can be really difficult to REALLY get to know someone.

We've done it to ourselves.

Between Google, social media, find friends, subtweeting and subtexting, we've gotten to a place where we think we're forming deep, long lasting connections, but oftentimes they're actually superficial. We should be striving to make connections beyond emojis and lols, beyond what we can say in 140 characters or less, beyond what pops up when we type someone's name into a search engine to see what we can find.

The next time you're out with that person you say you want to get to know better, ask them something deep, something real. See what kind of a conversation happens. And if you don't know where to start, maybe these 31 questions will help.

1. How many times did you change your mind about your career before you figured out what you really wanted to do?

2. Who are you closer with, your mom or your dad? Why do you think that is?

3. Who was the first person you ever loved?

4. What are five words you instinctually use to describe yourself?

5. What scares you the most about the future?

6. Do you think you'd make a good parent? Why or why not?

7. If/when you do become a parent, what is something you will take away from the way your parents raised you?

8. And what is something that you absolutely WON'T take away from the way you were raised?

9. Do you believe in heaven? Why or why not?

10. What is something you compromised on in a relationship that you wish you hadn't?

11. What is something you refused to compromise about in a relationship that you wish you would have?

12. How would your best friends describe you?

13. What would your friends who you've grown apart from say about you?

14. Do you think love is something you can't control, or something you choose to do?

15. Have you every cheated on someone?

16. What is your biggest fear about the future?

17. What makes you excited to get up in the morning?

18. What keeps you up at night?

19. What do you consider to be your biggest failure?

20. How do you handle your stress?

21. What holds you back from chasing things you really want?

22. What is something that scares you about yourself?

23. Which do you think is more important in a relationship, sexual compatibility or emotional compatibility?

24. Describe your worst/hardest break up.

25. Do you think we stay in love with some people forever?

26. Do you believe in staying friends with your exes? Why or why not?

27. Have you ever had to remove toxic people from your life? How did you do it?

28. Where do you go when you're sad?

29. What is one of your biggest regrets?

30. Do you think we only get one soulmate in life, or several?

31. Do you think if younger you met you today, they'd be proud of who you are?

12

50 Sexy Questions To Ask A Girl If You Want To Know What She's Like In Bed

Sylvie Quinn

1. What does it feel like when you orgasm?

2. What do you need to happen for your orgasm to be absolutely mind-blowing?

3. What's one thing that's made you feel unexpectedly good in bed?

4. What's one thing that you hesitated to try during sex but ended up *loving*?

5. Are you a screamer? A moaner?

6. How did you learn to masturbate, and how old were you when you first succeeded?

7. What's your favorite method for getting yourself off?

8. What types of props have you used during sex?

9. What's your favorite kind of foreplay?

10. Have you ever repurposed a regular household item as a sex toy? If so, which one(s)?

11. If you had to choose, would you be a dominatrix or a submissive?

12. What's the nastiest thing you've ever said to get someone off?

13. What's the dirtiest thing you've ever sexted someone?

14. Do you like taking naked photos of yourself?

15. What's your personal record for the number of times you've had sex in one night?

16. What's the most daring place you've done it in public?

17. What sexual position makes you feel most like yourself?

18. In what position to you orgasm most reliably?

19. What's your favorite way to get a man off?

20. What's your favorite blowjob technique?

21. What makes you wet without fail?

22. What's your favorite strategy for getting him to cum asap?

23. How many different ways have you orgasmed?

24. What, if anything, makes you feel vulnerable when you're naked with someone?

25. What makes you feel comfortable when you're naked someone?

26. What's your favorite part of a man's body?

27. What's your favorite part of your own body?

28. What's the dirtiest dream you've ever had?

29. Have you ever made an erotic fantasy come true?

30. If you had one day left to live, how would you want it?

31. Who's the one person in this world you wish you could fuck?

32. What's the dirtiest thought you've ever had?

33. What's the sexiest compliment you've ever gotten?

34. What's the sexiest compliment you've ever given?

35. How do you like your pussy to be licked?

36. Do you like it rough or gentle?

37. What's the most sexually daring thing you've ever done?

38. What's the naughtiest thing you've ever asked someone to do to you?

39. How would you describe the taste of your own vagina?

40. What does your ideal penis look like?

41. How seriously do you take your sex life?

42. What turns you on the most about the opposite sex?

43. What is your hottest sexual memory?

44. What's your biggest sexual fear?

45. If you could take on any fictional character's personality in bed, who would you be?

46. What's your favorite sex toy to play with?

47. Have you ever had sex with two different people in one night?

48. How good are you at faking an orgasm? Show me…

49. How many different people have you had great sex with?

50. What's the one sex act you want to try before you die?

13

He's Not Your Forever Person Unless He Can Answer These 60 Questions

Holly Riordan

1. I would never watch a movie if _____ starred in it.

2. I think I look best in the color _____.

3. I'll never delete the _____ app from my phone.

4. Even though everyone else loves it, I can't stand _____.

5. The most upsetting celebrity death was _____.

6. I usually hate people with the name _____.

7. If you want to get me in the mood for sex, all you have to do is _____.

8. I had a million posters of _____ on my wall when I was little.

9. Even though it's childish, I still love to watch _____.

10. People make fun of me for the way I pronounce _____.

11. _____ gives me major anxiety.

12. _____ is my favorite social media platform for sharing selfies.

13. I cry every single time I hear the song _____.

14. If any celebrity couple could adopt me, I'd want it to be _____.

15. _____ is the sexiest accent in the world.

16. Some day, I want to own _____ dogs.

17. The dumbest reason I've ever broken up with someone was because _____.

18. My favorite Disney movie is _____.

19. If I had to have plastic surgery, I would get _____.

20. When I take a selfie, _____ is my go-to pose.

21. The longest I've been on a plane was for _____ hours.

22. _____ is the best meal I can make without a cookbook.

23. The best celebrity impression I can do is _____.

24. _____ is the nickname that my parents always call me by.

25. My very first job was at a _____.

26. I can't stand the smell of _____.

27. _____ is my favorite brand of beer.

28. _____ is my favorite brand of cereal.

29. I hate the way my _____ looks.

30. _____ is the habit that I've been trying to break for years.

31. When I wake up, the first thing I do is _____.

32. I hate when my boss asks me to _____.

33. _____ is my favorite Christmas song.

34. The _____ emoji annoys the hell out of me.

35. I've always wanted to get a tattoo of _____.

36. I hate when people have tattoos of _____.

37. I need at least _____ hours of sleep to function properly.

38. I hate when people have their _____ pierced.

39. If I buy a candle, it's going to smell like _____.

40. My dream date would consist of going to _____.

41. _____ was the most exciting moment of my life.

42. _____ was the greatest thing that I've ever read.

43. My favorite type of porn involves _____.

44. I always want to throw up after eating _____.

45. I don't understand why people go to _____ on vacation.

46. If I could own a wild animal, it would be a _____.

47. I hate watching _____ with you.

48. I eat _____ meals per day.

49. Everybody hates _____, but I love it.

50. The best compliment I've ever been given was _____.

51. The most embarrassing thing I own is a _____.

52. I miss _____, but I won't text them.

53. I'm super turned off by _____.

54. My favorite part of my body is my _____.

55. _____ is the insect that I'll run far away from.

56. I always forget to _____.

57. I would rather live in _____ than where I live now.

58. _____ was the teacher that had the biggest impact on me.

59. _____ is the first thing on my bucket list.

60. I love you, because _____.

14

23 Borderline Genius Questions To Ask If You Want To Know What He Really Thinks About You

Erin Cossetta

1. What fictional character do I remind you of?

2. Do you think our zodiac signs accurately describe our personalities?

3. If we were going to have a dinner party and could invite anyone living or dead, who do you think we'd have the most fun with?

4. What do you hope your life is like when you're retired?

5. What scares you about me?

6. What's the weirdest things you like about me?

7. What do you want to do on your next vacation, if money weren't an object?

8. Which actors would play us in a movie?

9. What's the first thing you think about in the morning?

10. What's the last thing you think about before you fall asleep?

11. In your opinion, what's the best date we've ever had?

12. What's one question you'd love to ask a psychic if you found out one was really real?

13. What's a song that makes you think about us?

14. How do you think your mind works differently than mine?

15. Who is your all time favorite couple, and why?

16. What kinds of people can you not stand?

17. What kind of girl did you think you would end up with when you were younger?

18. When have you had the most fun with me?

19. Who is the first fictional character you remember having a crush on?

20. How would your life be different if you made an extra $5,000 every month?

21. What's the best compliment someone has ever given you?

22. When are you the most comfortable?

23. If we were animals, what kind of animals would we be?

15

100 Good Questions To Ask A Guy That Will Bring You Closer Together

Marisa Donnelly

1. What is one thing that brings a smile to your face, no matter the time of day?

2. What's is one thing that you're proud of?

3. What makes you laugh?

4. When you're feeling super lazy, what's your guilty pleasure Netflix show?

5. What's the scariest thing you've ever done?

6. What is one memory you have from childhood?

7. What's the best thing about your life right now?

8. What is one thing that you're thankful for?

9. What's one thing that you fear?

10. If you could only watch one movie for the rest of your life, what would it be?

11. Can you tell me one thing, big or small, that you've never told anyone else?

12. If you were forced to leave your home and move to a county you've never been before, what are three things that you'd take with you?

13. What's a favorite memory with a pet/animal?

14. Who are you closest to in your family?

15. What's your family like?

16. What's your favorite flavor of ice cream?

17. What's your favorite joke?

18. What's the stupidest thing you've ever done?

19. If you could rewrite your past, what's one thing you'd change?

20. What do you think your best physical feature is?

21. What's one thing about yourself, personality-wise, that you like?

22. When you're feeling down, who or what is your biggest go-to person or activity?

23. If you could only eat one food for the rest of your life, what would it be?

24. What's one thing you're super passionate about?

25. If you had to lose one of your five senses, which would you give up and why?

26. What's the hardest thing, physically, you've ever done?

27. What's the hardest thing, mentally, you've ever done or been through?

28. What's the best part about your job?

29. What's one thing that defines who you are?

30. If tomorrow was your last day on earth, what would you do in your last 24 hours?

31. What do you believe in, generally or faith-wise?

32. If you had to describe yourself in three words, what would they be?

33. Where's the coolest place you've ever been/traveled to?

34. What's one thing people would never know about you just by looking at you?

35. What's one thing about the opposite sex that you're attracted to?

36. What are three qualities you look for in a potential date?

37. What's the sweetest thing you've ever done for a girl?

38. How would others describe you?

39. What's your all-time favorite memory?

40. What are your parents/step-parents/guardians/people who raised you like?

41. What's your go-to alcoholic drink?

42. What would be your ideal first date?

43. If you could have three wishes, what would they be?

44. If you could a full 24 hours without any work or obligations, a day to just do whatever you wanted, what would you do?

45. What is the best compliment you've ever received?

46. What is something you're talented at?

47. What's your favorite college memory?

48. What is your best friend like?

49. If you could live anywhere in the world, where would you live?

50. What's one thing you want to do before you die?

51. If someone gave you a million dollars right now, what would you spend it on?

52. Have you ever made a decision that changed your entire life? If so, what was it?

53. What's your favorite thing to do on the weekends?

54. What's your zodiac sign? And do you think it describes you?

55. What's your biggest regret?

56. What can always put you in a good mood?

57. What's your guilty pleasure snack, drink, or junk food?

58. If you were forced to eat fast food for your every meal, what would be your top two places?

59. What's one thing you wish you could change about your-self?

60. If you had the option to hit restart and begin life all over again, would you?

61. Have you ever lost someone close to you? What were they like?

62. What's your favorite social media profile?

63. What's one thing that totally relaxes you when you're stressed?

64. What's a random hobby you've always wanted to try but never have?

65. When was the last time you cried, and why did you?

66. What scares you the most about the future?

67. Do you want to have children someday?

68. What do you imagine your future family will be like?

69. Have you ever done or accomplished something you never thought you could? What was it?

70. What's one thing you could never live without?

71. Who is one person you could never live without?

72. What's your favorite vacation place?

73. Would you rather go out or stay in on a Saturday night?

74. What's your favorite quote, line of poetry, or sentence?

75. What's your favorite family memory?

76. What's one thing that helps you decide you can trust someone?

77. Have you been in love before?

78. How would you explain what 'love' is?

79. Have you ever gotten your heart broken?

80. What's one thing you've learned about yourself from a past relationship?

81. What's your biggest pet peeve?

82. What's one thing that's a total turn off?

83. What's one thing that's a total turn on?

84. What's the craziest thing you've ever done for a girl?

85. What's your go-to drink/food/activity when you're sick and in bed?

86. What's the scariest thing that ever happened to you as a kid?

87. Who in your family, immediate or extended, are you the most similar to?

88. Where do you see yourself in five years?

89. What's your favorite song or artist?

90. What would be your dream job?

91. If you were writing a book about your life, what would the title be?

92. What's your favorite word?

93. What keeps you up at night?

94. What's your go-to phrase?

95. What's one silly, little-kid item that you still have somewhere hidden in your room?

96. Who is someone that's impacted your life or helped you become who you are?

97. What's one thing you want to achieve before you die?

98. What's your favorite book?

99. What's one thing, silly or serious, that you're guilty of?

100. What makes you blissfully, completely, smile-from-ear-to-ear happy?

16

50 Questions That Will Make You Fall Even Deeper In Love With Your Person

Holly Riordan

1. If you could speak to anyone in heaven, who would it be?

2. What memory do you replay the most in your mind?

3. Do you have any reoccurring dreams or nightmares?

4. At what age did you learn the most about yourself?

5. When was the last time you were disappointed in yourself?

6. Is there someone that you'll *never* forgive?

7. Which time period do you like the best, aesthetically speaking?

8. In what ways have you grown over the course of your life?

9. Do you think your parents are proud of where you are in life?

10. Is there a teacher that you wish you could call up and thank?

11. What's the worst physical pain that you've ever suffered through?

12. What couple (that you personally know) do you look up to?

13. What scent reminds you of your childhood?

14. What *don't* you regret that you probably should?

15. What's the most intimate thing a couple could do together?

16. Which song lyric has had the biggest impact on you?

17. Do you believe in ghosts, aliens, or any mythical creatures?

18. When do you feel the most attractive?

19. What's the nicest thing you've ever done for someone else?

20. What unanswerable question bothers you the most?

21. What do you think the best part of being married is?

22. Have you ever had a premonition that came true?

23. At what age did you start to consider yourself an adult?

24. What is the meanest thing your inner voice tells you?

25. Do you consider yourself a spiritual person?

26. What do you think your purpose in life is?

27. Were you ever tempted to cheat on a past partner?

28. What do you do when you're feeling lonely?

29. What type of animal would you like to be reincarnated as?

30. Do you believe every life has an equal value?

31. Do you daydream more about the future or your past?

32. What would instantly make you fall out of love with someone?

33. Do you believe you're going to be a good parent?

34. What scares you the most about growing old?

35. Do you like the sound of your name?

36. Which celebrity do you think you'd be BFFs with?

37. Do you believe in fortune tellers and tarot cards?

38. How long did it take you to learn to love yourself?

39. What do you think the afterlife consists of?

40. Have you ever manipulated someone to get what you wanted?

41. Do you believe in love at first sight or do you think it takes time to grow?

42. Which celebrity death impacted you the most?

43. Do you write in script or print?

44. Which wild animal do you wish you could keep as a pet?

45. Do you believe in destiny?

46. If you had to get a tattoo to honor someone, who would it be?

47. Do you feel like anything is missing from your life?

48. What's the most childish thing you still love to do?

49. What bad habit have you managed to break?

50. Do you believe success comes in the form of money or happiness?

17

32 Deeply Honest Questions You Shouldn't Be Afraid To Ask Your Significant Other

Kendra Syrdal

1. "Why do you love me?"

2. "When do I challenge you the most?"

3. "How could I be a better partner to you?"

4. "What do you miss most about someone from your past?"

5. "How have we changed since we first started dating?"

6. "What is your favorite memory of our relationship?"

7. "What is your least favorite memory of our relationship?"

8. "Is there anything you don't feel like you can talk to me about?"

9. "How have I improved your life?"

10. "What could do to make your life better?"

11. "What is something you are hesitant to tell me about my personality?"

12. "When did you know you could trust me?"

13. "How do you think we could communicate better as a couple?"

14. "What is your favorite thing we do together?"

15. "Have you had to sacrifice things in order to be with me?"

16. "How do you handle jealousy?"

17. "When do I make you laugh the hardest?"

18. "Has there ever been a moment where we just had to agree to disagree?"

19. "When have you been enormously proud of me?"

20. "When did you realize you were falling in love with me?"

21. "Have I ever disappointed you?"

22. "What has surprised you most about this relationship?"

23. "What do you consider to be my most attractive quality?"

24. "Has there ever been a time where you questioned us?"

25. "And if yes, how did we overcome that?"

26. "How do you still love me when I'm not my best?"

27. "What is something I influenced you to do?"

28. "If we did break up, what would you miss most about me?"

29. "How is this relationship different than your previous relationships?"

30. "Why were you drawn to me when we first started dating?"

31. "What will you always remember about me as a partner?"

32. "What can I do to help strengthen our relationship?"

18

45 Personal Questions To Ask Someone If You Want To Test How Compatible You Really Are

Rania Naim

1. Where would you like to be in 5 years?

2. What was the experience that impacted you the most in your life?

3. What type of relationship did you have with your parents?

4. Would you be with someone who doesn't have the same beliefs as you?

5. How would your best friends describe you?

6. Do you usually follow your heart or your head?

7. Would you put your family or your friends first if you had to choose one?

8. What did your last relationship teach you?

9. What do you think of online dating?

10. Do you prefer dating just one person and see where it goes or dating multiple people until you make a decision?

11. What are the qualities you're looking for in someone you want to grow old with?

12. What are you most grateful for in your life?

13. If you could change anything about your past, what would it be?

14. What's the one thing you would like to change about yourself today and why?

15. If a psychic could tell you what will happen in the future, what would you want to know?

16. If you knew that you only had one year to live, what would you change in your life?

17. If money and career were no object, what would you really be doing?

18. What do you do when you don't get something you worked really hard for?

19. Do you hold grudges or do you forgive easily?

20. What are some of your favorite quotes and why do you relate to them?

21. Where do you go when you need some inspiration?

22. Who is the first person you call when you're in trouble?

23. Which fictional character do you believe is the most like yourself?

24. What is the craziest thing that you've done with someone?

25. Do you like someone you're interested in to pursue you or do you prefer to do the chasing?

26. What is the best advice you've ever been given?

27. If you could marry anyone in the world, who would it be and why?

28. Do you think confessions make a relationship stronger?

29. Did you ever judge someone for the dark secrets they told you?

30. What is your dream vacation and who would you take with you?

31. What is one thing you've always wanted to cross off your bucket list, but haven't yet?

32. Would you ever just quit everything and start over in a new country?

33. Would you relocate for love?

34. How do you feel about staying friends with exes?

35. What's your love language?

36. If you could choose one superpower, what would it be and why?

37. What is your biggest regret in life so far?

38. Who is your role model?

39. What was your favorite romantic moment and why?

40. What is your favorite childhood memory?

41. Are you still in touch with your childhood friends?

42. What do you do when you're angry?

43. What are your beliefs on God?

44. Do you believe in soul mates?

45. How long does it take you to really trust someone?

19

55 Questions All Siblings Should Be Able To Answer About Each Other

Maya Kachroo-Levine

1. What was their most prized childhood possession?

2. What did they do as a little kid that was super embarrassing?

3. What sports did they play growing up?

4. What did they want to be when they grew up?

5. What kind of treats did they always want on their birthday?

6. What was their favorite book as a kid?

7. What do you do that still drives them totally crazy?

8. What is something that completely changed about them as they got older?

9. What was the one thing about them everyone else commented on when they were young?

10. Where else did they apply to college?

11. Who was the person they thought they were going to end up with in high school?

12. Who did they take to prom?

13. What's one of their go-to comfort foods?

14. What's the best place they've ever traveled?

15. What outfit did they wear all the time as a kid that your parents still talk about?

16. Which one of your friends did they have a huge crush on?

17. What's their favorite season?

18. What do they always disagree with your parents about?

19. What were they actually like in high school? Stoner? Goody two-shoes? Athlete?

20. What's one present they'll always be happy to receive?

21. What is their dream job now?

22. Do they want to get married?

23. Do they want kids, or a family?

24. Do they want to live in the same city as you one day?

25. What was their worst fear as a kid? Has it changed?

26. Do they have an athletic goal they've always wanted to achieve? (Like hiking the Appalachian trail or running a marathon?)

27. What are their weaknesses?

28. What is your go-to activity when you are reunited with them?

29. What's their guilty pleasure TV show?

30. What was one embarrassing obsession of their childhood?

31. How do they like their eggs?

32. Are they team Bloody Mary, or team mimosa?

33. If you guys could take a sibling trip, no parents or other relatives or significant others, where would you go?

34. Are they super organized, messy/neat and fairly laid back, or a complete slob?

35. What is one giveaway sign that they are really stressed, really hungry, or really tired?

36. Are they good with technology?

37. Are they book smart or street smart?

38. Are they a chocolate person?

39. Do they prefer dogs or cats?

40. Do they want to live in the city, country, or suburbs of a city?

41. What kind of music do you both like to listen to (because it's what your parents also listened to)?

42. What did they (or do they currently) major in in college?

43. Are they competitive, or are they the type of person who's always supporting others?

44. Were they a teacher's pet in elementary school?

45. Were they obsessed with their birthday growing up, or did they not like all the attention?

46. On a scale of one to 10, how much do they care about social media?

47. If you're the older sibling, do(es) your younger sibling(s) feel like they're always trying to fill your shoes? Or have they always known they wanted to be doing something different?

48. If you're the younger sibling, do(es) your older sibling(s) feel like they need to be guiding you every step of the way, or do you they take a more hands-off approach?

49. Do they love to read, or would they rather spend Friday night catching up on their favorite shows?

50. When they were growing up, were they an introvert or an extrovert?

51. Are they an introvert or extrovert now?

52. What is something they have in common with your parents that you don't share?

53. What is something you share with your parents (or other siblings) that they don't?

54. What is one thing they wanted to accomplish when they were younger that they have now hit out of the park?

55. What are you most proud of them for?

20

31 Enlightening Questions You Should Ask Your Parents While You Still Can

Kendra Syrdal

Being a parent is arguably one of the most challenging and most eye-opening experiences a person can have in their lifetime. They say it shapes you and molds you and ultimately changes the person you are for the rest of your life. While not all of us are lucky enough to have our parents still around, those of us who are should be taking advantage of all of the knowledge they have to share.

When you have some time, sit down with your parents and have a conversation with them. Ask them questions (like maybe one from down below) and really absorb what they have to say. You might be surprised at the answers you get, and it will absolutely strengthen the already incredible bond you share with someone who was so instrumental in your life, and raising you to be the person who you are today.

1. Tell me the story about my birth.

2. What kind of parent did you think you would be? And what kind of parent do you think you ended up being?

3. What was your biggest fear about raising kids?

4. What do you think I missed out on growing up when I did, versus had I grown up when you did?

5. Did you ever want more children?

6. What's your favorite thing about being a parent?

7. What's something about you that has nothing to do with family that you love about yourself?

8. What are your goals now that you aren't my caretaker anymore?

9. What was something you took away from how you grew up that you either wanted to replicate, or never do as a parent?

10. Did your views on religion/sex/family dynamics/politics change because of having kids?

11. How would you describe yourself to a complete stranger?

12. What is something I still do not know about you?

13. What is something that happened when I was growing up that completely shaped the way you raised me afterward?

14. Tell me about when you found out you were going to have me.

15. Is there something about me that is completely identical to you? Is there something about me that is completely the opposite of you?

16. What was the hardest part about me growing up?

17. Do you think I will/would make a good parent?

18. Did you struggle with the decision to have kids?

19. What was I like as a baby?

20. Who was your biggest inspiration as a caretaker?

21. What is your favorite part about yourself?

22. What challenges did you and my father/mother/your partner have to work through as co-parents?

23. How did being a parent affect your relationships outside of the one with me?

24. Tell me about a time when you really hated being a parent.

25. Was there ever a time you really doubted your ability to raise me?

26. What do you do differently now that I'm grown up?

27. Are you proud of who I've become?

28. How did you pick my name?

29. Tell me about a favorite memory from my childhood.

30. What made you feel ready to be a parent?

31. Describe the difference between the love you have for a partner and friends, and the love you have for your children.

21

40 Creepy Would You Rather Questions To Help You Determine How Disturbed Your Friends Are

Holly Riordan

1. Would you rather hear the voices of dead people or see their ghosts?

2. Would you rather cut off your own arm or gouge out your own eye?

3. Would you rather be convicted of a crime you didn't commit or kill and get away with it?

4. Would you rather be abducted by aliens or possessed by a demon?

5. Would you rather live a (miserable) eternal life or go straight to hell tomorrow?

6. Would you rather have sex with a family member or with a dead body?

7. Would you rather be stuck on an island with a killer or stuck in the ocean with hungry sharks?

8. Would you rather be blind or see spirits everywhere you go?

9. Would you rather experience sleep paralysis every single night or see occasional hallucinations during the day?

10. Would you rather dip your foot in acid or set in on fire?

11. Would you rather be tortured by a ghost or an alien?

12. Would you rather spend the night at a haunted hotel or inside an insane asylum?

13. Would you rather fall to your death or be buried alive?

14. Would you rather bleed from your ears or your eyes?

15. Would you rather be stuck in the woods with Slenderman or with Hannibal Lecter?

16. Would you rather hear strange noises in the middle of the night or see strange shadows on your wall?

17. Would you rather run over a body and see who you hit or drive away?

18. Would you rather kill an evil human or an innocent animal?

19. Would you rather wake up with an IV in a creepy hospital or chained to a radiator in an empty room?

20. Would you rather see Freddy Krueger in your dreams or Norman Bates at a motel?

21. Would you rather be eaten alive by a bear or by a wolf?

22. Would you rather be drowned in a bathtub or trapped in a burning building with no way of escaping?

23. Would you rather find out you were a vampire or a werewolf?

24. Would you rather be the victim of a serial killer or turn into a serial killer?

25. Would you rather wake up without any hands or without any genitals?

26. Would you rather watch your parent or your partner die slowly?

27. Would you rather die of starvation or of overeating?

28. Would you rather find a human head or a human hand in your kitchen?

29. Would you rather lose your mind or all your limbs?

30. Would you rather find a dead body in your backyard or just the guts?

31. Would you rather be kidnapped for six months and survive or die without any psychological damage?

32. Would you rather eat human skin or naw on the bones?

33. Would you rather murder your best friend brutally or be murdered by your best friend?

34. Would you rather eat the dead flesh of your mother or your father?

35. Would you rather be shot by a stranger or by someone close to you?

36. Would you rather get struck in the stomach by a bullet or swallow rat poison?

37. Would you rather get turned on by blood or by insects?

38. Would you rather eat a dead rat or live spiders?

39. Would you rather be attacked by a clown or a toy doll?

40. Would you rather date someone hot who has killed before or be alone for the rest of your life?

22

100 Big Questions Successful People Never Stop Asking Themselves

Mélanie Berliet

1. If I were to lose everything today, what would I do tomorrow?

2. Is this really where I want to be?

3. How did I get here, exactly?

4. Is there enough love in my life?

5. How can I be more attentive to those I care about, and more valuable those who need me most?

6. What will my life look like ten years down the line if I stay the current course?

7. Am I prepared to reinvent myself if need be?

8. How would others describe me?

9. How would I describe myself in a few sentences, as honestly as possible?

10. Is the work I do enriching?

11. Is this really the best I can do at [insert any given task]?

12. Am I taking enough risks?

13. Am I doing a sufficient job tuning out all the noise?

14. How can I be more present?

15. Am I as healthy as I could be?

16. What do I really gain from [insert bad habit]?

17. Is this the right city/town/suburb/place for me?

18. What does my Happily Ever After look like, within reason?

19. What practical measures can I take to get to my Happy Place?

20. What excites me most?

21. Who am I able to be my authentic self around?

22. How can I infuse my surroundings with more positive energy?

23. Which causes do I truly believe in, and what can I do to get behind them?

24. What are my main goals, and the actionables for achieving these objectives?

25. How can I actually make some small but important difference in the lives of others?

26. Which activities make me feel sincerely fulfilled?

27. What are some useful life hacks I can apply to my daily life?

28. How can I embrace innovation?

29. What is the best solution to [insert daily frustration]?

30. What is the best workaround for [insert looming predicament]?

31. What can I learn from each and every one of my failures?

32. What am I really doing with my life—on a micro and macro level?

33. What can I do to make my daily existence yet more rewarding?

34. What would the me from five years ago think of the me today?

35. How can I respond better to life mishaps, big and small?

36. How can I prepare myself better for the future?

37. Is this a smart decision?

38. Is my heart really in this?

39. What would [insert someone you admire] do in this scenario?

40. Do I expect too much?

41. How can I work towards being a better person?

42. Can I honestly claim to have a sense of purpose?

43. Am I leading a meaningful life?

44. What is my authentic truth?

45. Am I giving others enough credit when due?

46. How can I be kinder to strangers day to day?

47. How can I share the wealth of knowledge I've acquired thus far?

48. How can I become yet more skilled at my trade and more specialized in my areas of expertise?

49. Am I taking enough vacation?

50. Do I work for and with people I genuinely respect?

51. How can I control my emotions better?

52. Am I doing enough to celebrate the achievements of others?

53. What more can I do to tame envy and other destructive emotions when they strike?

54. How can I make more time for laughter, lightheartedness, hobbies, and fun?

55. How can I overcome my greatest fears?

56. How can I spread more joy?

57. Am I building a life with the right person?

58. What can I do to make a friend smile in the next hour?

59. How can I improve a stranger's circumstances today?

60. How can I love my family members better?

61. What more can I do to appreciate all the little things and embrace all the tiny moments worth noting?

62. What can I do to lead a more fulfilling life overall?

63. Am I decent?

64. Am I being honest with myself?

65. What self-care initiatives can I incorporate into my daily life moving forward?

66. What can I do to shrink my ego and grow a bigger heart?

67. Am I valuing experiences over the acquisition of stuff?

68. Is this world a better place because I'm in it?

69. What can I do to strengthen my weaknesses, and to mend the broken parts of my soul?

70. Am I expending enough energy on worthwhile endeavors?

71. Am I treating every single person I interact with respectfully?

72. How can I work towards living more mindfully?

73. What does a 'good life' entail, in my opinion?

74. What traits in others do I most aspire to replicate in myself?

75. How can I contribute more to my community?

76. What can I do to make the world a better place, even if only in some minuscule way?

77. Is this what I want?

78. How can I train myself to be more accepting of others?

79. Am I leading a healthy, balanced life?

80. In what situations do I truly excel?

81. What is my honest definition of 'success'?

82. How can I position myself better to achieve my objectives?

83. What can I do to impart some of the wisdom I've acquired on younger generations?

84. What can I do to learn more from others?

85. What steps can I take to ignore trivial distractions in favor of focusing on the bigger picture?

86. How can I exercise more self control?

87. Am I operating from a place of good intentions?

88. Am I aware and accepting of my own limitations?

89. Is there something more I can do for the people I love right this second?

90. Are my priorities in line with my personal values?

91. Have I earned the respect of others?

92. How can I maintain a sense of perspective at all times?

93. What can I do to recuperate faster from life's setbacks?

94. Does anyone look up to me?

95. Does my life to date qualify as an honorable one?

96. Am I doing my best to withhold judgment?

97. Have I given my parents and others good reason to be proud of me?

98. What more should I be doing?

99. Can I honestly claim to love the person I am?

100. Am I asking enough questions?

23

27 Questions You Should Ask If You Actually Want To Get To Know Someone

Kendra Syrdal

1. Do you believe in nurture? Or do you favor nature?

2. Have you ever had a reoccurring dream? What do you think it meant/represented?

3. If you were in complete control of the circumstances, how would you want to die?

4. How would your best friend describe you if asked?

5. What was one of the most ridiculous things you believed as a kid, and how did you find out the truth about it?

6. Where and when are you your best self?

7. When you picture your most fulfilled, happy self, how would you describe what you envision?

8. What was the first thing you were really good at?

9. If you could trade lives with anyone for 24 hours, who would it be and why?

10. How do you want people to remember you?

11. Do you believe that we really CAN choose to be happy? Why or why not?

12. If you could give 15 year-old you one piece of advice, what would you say?

13. Do you feel like you are proud of the person you've become?

14. When you hear the term "sparking joy" what comes to mind?

15. Who is your favorite person other than yourself?

16. What is your biggest fear?

17. What's your greatest strength/asset?

18. What about your biggest weakness/personal obstacle?

19. How would you describe the word 'chill' when talking personality wise?

20. Do you think you are a 'chill' person? Why or why not?

21. If you could go back to school, what classes would you take (regardless of major) and why?

22. Do you think that everything happens because of chance, or do you think we're more in control that we give ourselves credit for?

23. What kind of friend do you try to be? And "a good one" is not an acceptable answer.

24. How much do you care about how other people think of you?

25. If you weren't worried about the consequences and knew everything would go back to "normal" after, what would you do for 24 hours?

26. Describe your soulmate.

27. What to you is the perfect way to spend a weekend?

31 Questions To Ask If You Want To Reinvent Yourself But Aren't Sure Where To Start

Chrissy Stockton

The allure of reinvention is one of the things that makes frustration bearable. We know there's always time for another chance. With the right tools we can turn around and build a more exciting life tomorrow. If you're itching for something new but not sure what it looks like, spend some time with these questions:

1. What makes me feel happiest?

2. What makes me feel most frustrated?

3. If the obstacle of money was removed, how would my life look different?

4. What other obstacles are between me and the life I think I want?

5. What could I start doing today that would remove just one of these things in a year?

6. What productive activities do I spend time doing for no other reason than they makes me happy?

7. What do I do better than anyone else?

8. What traits and values do the people I most admire have in common?

9. What traits and values do the people I hate the most have in common?

10. How much money do I *really* need to be happy?

11. If physical location, education, money (and actually having to land the job) weren't factors, what would I do for work?

12. How would I most like someone to describe me?

13. What things do I only do because it makes other people validate me?

14. What is the worst thing someone could say about me?

15. What activities did I do on the best day of my life?

16. What did I like doing when I was younger that I've lost touch with?

17. What would I be most sad to have never tried?

18. What would I title my memoir if I had to write one right now?

19. What would I *rather* title it, even if the theme doesn't quite fit me (yet)?

20. What is the most important way I want my life to be different in 10 years?

21. What do I most look forward to each day?

22. When was the last time I felt a big rush of satisfaction?

23. What do people tell me I would be good at?

24. Which habit do I most wish I could work on getting rid of this year?

25. What would happen if I read for just 20 minutes each evening?

26. What do I want to be remembered for?

27. How can I incorporate breaks from my phone into my daily or weekly schedule?

28. What would help me let go of past hurts in my life?

29. Could I spend just five minutes each day following along with a yoga channel on YouTube?

30. What is the best compliment someone could give me?

31. In what ways is the best version of myself different from the current version of myself?

25

35 Questions To Help You Find Your Calling

Rania Naim

1. What motivates or inspires you?

2. What do you do well naturally and effortlessly?

3. What is the one thing that you do that you always get positive feedback on?

4. What's the one thing that's missing in your current life and career?

5. Do you feel like what you're doing right now is making you happy or bringing you closer to happiness?

6. If you didn't have to worry about money, what would you really be doing?

7. What did you want to be when you were a kid? What was your childhood dream?

8. Who is your role model or who do you look up to when it comes to living a passionate or purposeful life? And what are they doing differently?

9. What do you want to be remembered for? What's the message you want to leave behind?

10. What activities do you do that make you unaware of time and bring out the best in you?

11. What is the one thing that you won't get tired of doing every day?

12. What would you do if you knew you wouldn't fail?

13. Is fear the only thing holding you back from finding or living your calling?

14. How supportive are the people around you when it comes to living your passion?

15. Are you listening too much to them and ignoring your gut?

16. Do you believe you have what it takes to follow your passion?

17. If not, what are the tools you need to make you believe in yourself?

18. What is preventing you from following or finding you calling?

19. Are you confusing your job with your purpose?

20. What doesn't feel like work to you?

21. What do people tell you you're *exceptional* at?

22. What talent do you possess that you know sets you apart from everyone else?

23. Would you be able to downsize your expenses and lifestyle so you can truly do what you love?

24. Do you have friends or mentors who are living their calling? How did they do it?

25. Are you saying yes to opportunities and activities that you truly enjoy?

26. Are you connecting with people who are passionate about the same things you're passionate about?

27. Are you reading books on how to make them happen?

28. Are you actively trying to research how to get started?

29. If you were to quit your job and follow you passion, do you have enough savings to survive for a few months?

30. If not, how can you save up more so you can focus on living your passion?

31. Are you asking for advice or guidance?

32. Are you working on improving your skills or talents so you can stand out?

33. Are you mentally prepared to face rejections or setbacks until you make it happen?

34. Are you willing to ignore the naysayers and be your own source of motivation and encouragement?

35. What's the worst that could happen if you actually started living our passion?

26

40 Thought-Provoking Questions To Ask Yourself If You Want To Live An Emotionally Healthy Life

Kaitlyn Dunagan

1. Am I accomplishing goals beyond what is expected of me?

2. Are all my hobbies for pure enjoyment or do some of them contribute something to society for?

3. Do I ask for what I need even when it may cause conflict?

4. Am I generous to those who have nothing to give me?

5. Have I become comfortable with my life for the sake of self-preservation?

6. How am I challenging myself?

7. Am I challenging myself?

8. Do I stay silent when I should speak out against an injustice?

9. Am I taking advantage of those I love?

10. Are my loved ones taking advantage of me?

11. Why am I doing what I am doing?

12. Am I only doing [insert goal here] in order to be considered successful by others?

13. Do I treat others in an ethical manner?

14. Did I make someone laugh or smile today?

15. Did I make myself laugh or smile today?

16. Am I assuming more than I am asking?

17. Am I overthinking every situation to the detriment of my relationships?

18. When I am in a rut, am I accepting myself for who I am in the present moment?

19. When I make mistakes, do I treat *myself* the way I would treat others?

20. When I make mistakes, do I treat *others* the way I would want to be treated?

21. Are the decisions I am making today going to negatively impact my future?

22. Am I okay with not knowing the answer to a difficult question?

23. Why do I feel embarrassed when I am wrong?

24. Is having the answer to a question more important than my emotional well-being?

25. In my work or relationship(s), do I ever 'dig deeper' or am I always settling for mediocrity?

26. Have I learned about a new topic?

27. Do I learn the bare minimum about a subject or do I increase my knowledge on a subject I have a decent grasp on?

28. Do I always make decisions based on my emotions?

29. Do I always make decisions based on logic?

30. What is the best way for me to grieve?

31. How does the way I grieve affect those I care about most?

32. When is it okay for me to be impulsive?

33. When would it benefit me the most to be more organized?

34. Do I believe people are naturally talented or that the success of others is a mix of hard work and (possibly) natural talent?

35. How am I engaging my senses on a daily basis?

36. On a scale of 1 to 10, how closed off am I to others?

37. On a scale of 1 to 10, how dependent am I on others?

38. How long has it been since I have had a creative project?

39. How much do I complain?

40. How many times do I remind myself to be grateful for what I have?

YOU MIGHT ALSO LIKE:

All The Words I Should Have Said **by Rania Naim**

101 Essays That Will Change The Way You Think **by Brianna Wiest**

Huh? A Book Of All The Questions Worth Asking **by Thought Catalog**

THOUGHT
CATALOG
Books